D0466784

The Forbidden Gospel

The
Forbidden
Gospel

J. Edgar Bruns

HARPER & ROW, PUBLISHERS

New York, San Francisco, London

To all who are not deceived
by the merchants of Utopia
and with gratitude
to H. W. R.

FIRST EDITION

Designed by Dorothy Schmiderer

Library of Congress Cataloging in Publication Data

Bruns, J Edgar, 1923–
   The forbidden Gospel.

   1. Jesus Christ—Biography—Apocryphal and legendary
literature. 2. Gnosticism. I. Title.
BT520.B83   1976   229'.8   75-9315
ISBN 0-06-061149-9

76 77 78 79 10 9 8 7 6 5 4 3 2 1

Contents

Preface

I HAVE BEEN INTERESTED in Gnosticism for some years as a natural result of my studies and publications on the fourth gospel. It became increasingly apparent to me that the scholarly world would begin to manifest a special interest in this religion which, though it appeared to have been smothered in the third century, has reappeared in various forms down through the centuries, for the simple reason that so much of its long-lost literature had been recovered from the Egyptian sands in the late 1940s and was now, after years of delay, beginning to appear in printed form. Scholars live on such discoveries. Without them they must keep trying to think of new ways to approach some old problem.

It did not, at first, occur to me that Gnosticism and its ancient teachers could ever interest the reading public at large but I realized I was mistaken, and why, when I came across Jacques Lacarrière's *Les Gnostiques* (1973). Here is a well informed and brilliantly written introduction for laymen like Lacarrière who find in Gnosticism a philosophy of life which makes sense to them because it looks at the world searchingly and concludes that it is an incurably diseased organism. I was particularly interested to note, at the time, that the great English novelist and poet Lawrence Durrell had written the preface to Lacarrière's book. My surprise was accordingly not as great as it might have been when I even more recently discovered that Durrell's latest novel turns on the impact Gnostic religion has on a group of sophisticated European contemporaries. The title of the book is *Monsieur: or the Prince of Darkness.* "Monsieur" is not, as you might think, Satan, but that god of the Jews whom the Gnostics regarded as the cruel and ignorant creator of our world.

This book of mine, conceived long before I knew of Lacarrière's or Durrell's interest in Gnosticism, attempts to bring to life the Jesus whom those long-ago Gnostics thought of as one of their own, and that picture of him which is left to us scattered throughout their literature. It is my assumption, now, that if Gnosticism is on its way to becoming a popular philosophy, the Gnostic Jesus, buried for so many centuries, cannot fail to evoke a matching appeal.

In quoting the New Testament I have generally followed the *RSV Common Bible* (An Ecumenical Edition). I have also referred to the following works in preparing this volume: J. H. Charlesworth's *The Odes of Solomon* (Oxford University Press); W. Schneemelcher's *New Testament Apocrypha* (The Westminster Press); J. Menard's *L'Evangile selon Philippe* (Letouzey et Ane); Morton Smith's *The Secret Gospel* (Harper & Row); *The Gospel of Thomas* (Harper & Row); and R. M. Grant's *Gnosticism* (Harper & Row).

J. Edgar Bruns

Introduction

THERE IS AN ALMOST bewildering number of characterizations of Jesus today: on the level of popular entertainment one can choose between the whimsical clown of *Godspell* and the strident social critic of *Jesus Christ Superstar*. In the more sober literary world we have the revolutionary Jesus of Brandon, the scheming Jesus of Schonfield, the mythical Jesus who is a phallic symbol of Allegro, and the real but equally phallic Jesus of Morton Smith. And these are but the most recent portrayals. If we want to know how people thought of Jesus before books were published for a wide audience—which means before the nineteenth century—we have to look at art; and what do we find? We have the Jesus of the catacombs who is clearly a man like the rest of us but who is, essentially, a wonder-worker; we have the Jesus of the dazzling mosaics of the later Roman empire who is clearly not a man like the rest of us but a superman of cosmic dimensions and cosmic power; we have the Jesus of the Renaissance who is a model for the anatomical perfection of the human body; and we have the Jesus of the seventeenth and eighteenth centuries who is, above all, a sentimental comforter.

And all of these Jesuses are based on "the evidence." The "evidence," of course, is the New Testament. After all, the Jesus we meet in all the four Gospels is certainly a wonder-worker at the same time that he is a man who eats and drinks and suffers and dies. The Jesus we meet in Paul, on the other hand, is "far above all rule and authority and power and dominion, and above every name that is named, not only in this age but in that which is to come" (Eph. 1:21). If we want to think of Jesus as beautiful we can recall what Luke tells us: "And the child grew and became strong, filled with wisdom" (Luke 2:40), and if we want to think of him as being sweet and gentle we need only refer to Matthew 11:29: "Take my yoke upon you and learn from me, for I am meek and humble of heart, and you will find rest for your souls." If, on the contrary, we prefer to see Jesus as an angry young (or middle-aged) man, we can point to his rough handling of the merchants in the temple and his devastating references to the Pharisees as hypocrites, blind guides, and whitened sepulchres. There is even room, for those who want to make the most of very little, for a sensuous Jesus: "the son of man came eating and drinking, and they say, 'behold a glutton and a drunkard, a friend of tax collectors and sinners'" (Matt. 11:19). Sex? Well, some people wonder just what all those women were doing in Jesus' company ("And they marveled that he was talking with a woman" [John 4:27]; "There were also women looking on from afar . . . and also many other women who came up with him to Jerusalem" [Mark 15:40]); others see something strange in the mention of "a young man" who followed him "with nothing but a linen cloth about his body" (Mark

14:51) and in the numerous allusions, in the Fourth Gospel, to "the disciple whom Jesus loved."

In short, on the basis of the "evidence" Jesus can be made out to be almost anything anyone wants him to be. To the gentle soul he is the teacher who bids his disciples to "turn the other cheek" when struck; to the malcontent he is the activist who said: "I came not to bring peace but a sword."

It is undoubtedly *because* Jesus has come down through history as being all these things that he has remained, even for this chaotic age, a religious symbol of tremendous significance. Attempts to "get behind" the "evidence" in order to discover a more "historical" Jesus have failed and it is not likely, at this time, that they can ever succeed. That is as it should be, for Jesus was, to begin with, an inspiration and that is what he remains. We have so many different portrayals of him because he has, from the very beginning, affected different men in different ways; that makes him the "man for all seasons" par excellence. It has long been known that there was yet another Jesus, a very important one in the earliest history of Christianity, who deserves to be considered today because, rightly or wrongly, he will appeal to large segments of modern man. In order to present this Jesus I have assembled "evidence," which is contemporaneous or nearly contemporaneous with the New Testament itself, in the form of a Gospel. This "evidence" comes from Christians who were later judged to be "heretics" and we must first say something about them.

Alienation is a key word in every analysis of our modern society. I do not think it is too much of an oversimplification to say that the roots of it lie in our urbanized, industrialized, materialistic, and over-populated world. All of these elements contribute toward an ever-increasing sense of impersonalization, artificiality, ruthless competition, and frustration. The ancient world, the world in which Christianity came upon the scene, was seized with the same malaise. True, it was not the technological world of today—though it was on the verge of becoming so—but it was a world of great cities (Alexandria had a population exceeding one million) and the kind of superficial prosperity which breeds great avarice and great inequities. The little man was but a tiny cog in an enormous wheel over which he had no control, much as he is today.

Such a state of affairs inevitably led to the con-clusion, on the part of the more thoughtful, that something was radically wrong with the world. Today the cause of the disease is sought in political and economic systems; two thousand years ago it was sought in the very fabric of the universe. Atheism, as we understand the term, did not exist in the ancient world; at least not to the extent that we can document it. If, consequently, the world appeared to be "in a mess" the fault must lie with higher powers than puny, miserable man. We can understand this reasoning because we know that many contemporaries abandon belief in the existence of a God for the very same reason. The ancients could not reject the idea of God though they faced the same problem; there had to be another kind of explanation.

For those who interest us here, the explanation went something like this: God, the true God, is totally beyond matter. He (we shall call him *he* as they did even though anything like a sexual characterization was ridiculous to them) was pure Mind, and as such he gave rise to other "spiritual" beings. The number of these varied from group to group among our philosophers, but invariably the "youngest" of these emanations, far enough removed from the "Father" to be curious and impetuous, made the terrible mistake of creating inferior beings, spiritual but outside the *Pleroma* (the *Pleroma* is the totality of the Father's issue). One of these creatures, an angel (often the Jewish god Yahweh), went a step further and created the material world in which we find ourselves. This "creator-god" was, of course, a benighted being, ignorant of the Father and self-deluded.

Unfortunately the divine emanation responsible for the first mistake was herself (for our friends usually designated this emanation as *Sophia* which means Wisdom, and as a woman, but with the same basic indifference to sex) caught up in the horrendous faux pas of her creature's creation and, fragmented, ended up dispersed throughout the cosmic mistake. It is the will of the Father, of course, that this mistake be reversed and that the *Pleroma* be reunited and the horrid consequence we know as the material world erased. But how can this come to be? Only by the redemption of Sophia.

And how can Sophia be redeemed? Only by, as it were, being put together again. And how can that happen? Only by her "parts" becoming aware of their true nature. And how can they come to that knowledge? Only through the instruction of a "redeemer" whom the Father will send—or has sent. Knowledge, therefore, is the most important factor in deliverance. Consequently, the ancient thinkers whose systematic explanation of cosmic disorder we have just reviewed, were called *Gnostics*, because in Greek, the lingua franca of antiquity, *Gnosis* means "knowledge."

Looking around the ugly world in which they (as we?) found themselves, the Gnostics discovered that the sensitivity of their fellowmen to the perversions of beauty, order, and justice which surrounded them, differed vastly. Some were intuitively aware of the situation; others became aware upon disclosure; still others neither saw nor wanted to see anything wrong with their ambience. What did this mean? Surely that some men had no "spark of life" in them, that is, no part of Sophia (which is to say, the *Pleroma*). These they called "wooden men" (Gr. *hylikoi*). Of and from them nothing was to be expected. Those who understood the situation intuitively (the "spirituals," Gr. *pneumatikoi*) felt called to instruct the great number of human beings "in the middle" (the *psychikoi* or "psychics"). Gnosticism was a truly missionary religion and it should be fairly evident that it had a certain affinity to the class-struggle aspect of Marxist-Leninism though for different reasons.

So much for the premises on which the Gnostics

acted. There were, to be sure, variations of this world view, but essentially it was as I have described it. The next question which poses itself is this: How is it that Jesus appears as the superlative "redeemer" in most of the Gnostic literature that survives?

III

For a long time it was thought that Gnosticism, as a religion, was a Christian "heresy"; something that would never have achieved articulation without the Gospels. As a result of an extraordinarily important discovery of Gnostic books in Egypt almost thirty years ago it is now nearly certain that the philosophy of life we have just reviewed was talked and written about before the Christian era. If Jesus became a Gnostic "hero" it was because the Gnostics saw in him someone they were looking for. But again the question: Why?

It all comes down, in fact, to the question: What did Jesus teach? And, in order to answer that, we have to be able to answer another question (by this time the reader must be acutely aware of the number of *questions* raised by our investigation); namely: What are our sources for the teaching of Jesus? The answer seems obvious enough: the Gospels! But no; it is not that simple. The Gospels themselves depend upon earlier material which was circulated both by word of mouth and in writing. Of this earlier material modern scholarship feels confident that it can identify three types: stories about the miracles of Jesus; collections of his sayings; and an account of his passion, death, and resurrection. Put simply, the Gospel of Mark is a combination of stories about the miracles of Jesus and an account of his passion and death; Matthew and Luke, who used the Gospel of Mark, have added collections of his sayings. John stands in a somewhat different category because although he is like Mark in having made use of a series of miracle stories and an account of the passion, death, and resurrection, he does not include the kinds of "sayings" incorporated into Matthew and Luke; rather, he adds a series of discourses, attributed to Jesus, which have much in common with the sort of teaching we find in Gnostic literature.

John, however, is generally recognized as a "late" gospel, that is, dating from the end of the first century. It was the Gospel of John which the Gnostics seized upon and they were the first Christains to comment upon it.

But it would be dishonest to say that it was only because of the Fourth Gospel that the Gnostics "latched on" to Jesus. The "sayings" of Jesus which found their way into Matthew and Luke (and even, though rarely, into Mark) contain teaching which makes little sense unless it is read in a Gnostic light. A striking example is the parable of the wheat and the tares (Matt. 13:24–30):

> The kingdom of heaven may be compared to a man who sowed good seed in his field; but while men were sleeping, his enemy came and sowed weeds among the wheat, and went away. So when the plants came up and bore grain, then the weeds appeared also. And the servants of the householder came and said to him: "Sir, did you not sow good

seed in your field? How then has it weeds?" He said to them: "An enemy has done this." The servants said to him: "Then do you want us to go and gather them?" But he said: "No, lest in gathering the weeds you root up the wheat along with them. Let both grow together until the harvest; and at harvest time I will tell the reapers, Gather the weeds first and bind them in bundles to be burned, but gather the wheat into my barn."

What do the good seed and the weeds stand for here? Clearly for different types of men; some men are "sown" by the Father and others by "the enemy." Accordingly some are destined for salvation (the householder's barn) and some for damnation (to be "burned"). This is Gnostic predestinarianism according to which mankind is divided into the three groups already described. Theoretically this classification is based on Gnostic speculations about creation (the ignorant and careless work of inferior powers, most often the Jewish god Yahweh), but it patently derives from simple observation of the varying kinds of human response to spiritual values. We find an echo of the idea of the good seed in 1 John 3:9: "No one born of God commits sin; for his [God's] seed abides in him," and of the tares in Matthew 15:13: "Every plant which my heavenly Father has not planted will be rooted up." Once it is understood that such statements have reference to individuals who are *constituted* good or bad, there is nothing "strange" or "enigmatic" as commentators like to say, about Matthew 7:6: "Do not give dogs what is holy; and do not throw your pearls before swine, lest they trample them under foot and turn to attack you." There are types (the *hylikoi*) who are incapable of understanding; do not waste time with them. On the other hand, there are always the psychics, those who may be brought to understanding and who are a proper object of concern (read "evangelization") and it is of these the parable in Matthew 22:2–14 speaks concluding, as it does, with the words: "Many are called but few are chosen."

In the context in which Matthew has set the saying: "Every plant which my heavenly father has not planted will be rooted up," it is made to refer to the Pharisees: "Let them alone; they are blind guides. And if a blind man leads a blind man, both will fall into a pit." The application, from a Gnostic point of view, is not inappropriate because those who believe the God of the Jews to be the true God are indeed blind. The religion of the Law and the prophets must not contaminate the truth, thought the Gnostic, and is this not what the parable at Mark 2:21–22 teaches? (The parable is common to the first three Gospels, which we call *synoptic* because in general they present the public life of Jesus in the same way, as if through "one and the same eye.") "No one sews a patch of raw cloth on an old garment; else the new patch tears away from the old, and a worse rent is made. And no one pours new wine into old wineskins; else the wine will burst the skins, and the wine is spilled and the skins will be ruined. But new wine must be put into fresh skins." Who, after all, is the "enemy" of the parable of the wheat and the tares? As already indicated, it is Yahweh, the God of the Jews. The average Bible commentary will say that it is Satan, but Satan, in both Jewish and Christian "orthodoxy" does not create men. May we think perhaps of a later harmonizing effort which substituted Satan for Yahweh in interpretation? The impulse to do so is strengthened by John 8:42–44: "If God were your (Jews) Father, you would love me, for I proceeded and came forth from God. . . . You are of your father the devil."

We have another interesting reference to origins in Matthew 11:16–19 (*see also* Luke 7, 31–35):

> But to what shall I compare this generation? It is like children sitting in the market places and calling to their playmates, "We piped to you and you did not dance; we wailed and you did not mourn." For John came neither eating nor drinking, and they say "He has a demon;" the Son of man came eating and drinking and they say "Behold a glutton and a drunkard, a friend of tax collectors and sinners." Yet wisdom [Gr. *Sophia*] is justified by her children.

The last verse here has always troubled readers and exegetes and some early scribes attempted to escape the difficulty by changing "children" to "works" which does not, of course, help very much. No help is really needed. In Gnostic thought Sophia is the creator of angels of whom Yahweh is preeminent, and Yahweh, of course, is the creator of our world. Sophia's children are ignorant of the truth and for this reason they cannot understand either John the Baptist or Jesus; insofar as they follow in Sophia's mistaken footsteps they endorse her work.

Just prior to the saying about the children of Sophia in Matthew we have another enigmatic statement which mentions John the Baptist (probably explaining why it is followed by the passage we have just studied):

> Truly I say to you, among those born of women there has risen no one greater than John the Baptist; yet he who is least in the kingdom of heaven is greater than he. From the days of John the Baptist until now the kingdom of heaven has suffered violence, and men of violence take it by force. For all the prophets and the law prophesied until John (Matt. 11:11–13).

Are not those who are "least" in the kingdom of heaven also born of woman? There must be some way in which they are *not* else how could the Baptist be the "greatest" so born? And what is the violence which must be used to gain possession of the kingdom of heaven? It is evidently a new imperative which was not recognized during the period when the Law and the prophets held sway. We should read this passage in conjunction with Matthew 12:29 with which it has in common the notion of violence: "Or how can one enter a strong man's house and plunder his goods, unless he first binds the strong man?" Under the Law and the prophets the kingdom of heaven was not taken because no violence was used. With the coming of Jesus all this has changed; those who use violence will win beatitude. Against whom, then, is the violence to be directed? Who if not he who kept men subdued through the Law and the prophets?

IV

There are many other "sayings" attributed to Jesus which are not to be found in the canonical Gospels but which may be found in the Gnostic *Gospel of Thomas*; these are even more obviously Gnostic in content and the fact is not denied by anyone who has written on the subject. Are we then to conclude that Jesus thought as a Gnostic? There is too much evidence against it for us to be able to say yes, but at the same time all the evidence, pro and con, taken together does not allow of any certainty. In point of time we cannot get behind the material in the canonical Gospels; there is nothing *earlier* of which we have examples, and if even the canonical material (and we are prescinding entirely from the Fourth Gospel) contains Gnostic-type teaching, as I hope I have shown, then who is to say what Jesus taught?

According to the canons of modern New Testament scholarship only those sayings of Jesus found in Matthew, Mark, Luke, and John are to be accepted as authentic which either reflect a break with the Judaism of the first century, do not reflect the Gentile milieu of the early Church, or create a difficulty for believers of a later generation. "Gnostic" sayings would, presumably, be ruled out on the grounds that they, more specifically than others, evoke the non–Jewish and even anti–Jewish ambience of the early Church. Very likely, but there is also the scholarly assumption that Jesus definitely stood for a break with the Judaism of his time. How far did he go in that? The answer is that we simply do not know and that, on any fair assessment, we cannot exclude the possibility of an attitude which *approached* that of the Gnostics and that, for such a reason, some of the very earliest material we possess reflects Gnostic assumptions. If it is a question of really trying to forge a link with the historical Jesus, the Gnostics have their own good case to make. Basilides, who taught in Egypt around 120, said that he was a disciple of Glaukias, "an interpreter of Peter"; Valentinus, who made a great impact on the Christian scene in Egypt and Rome some two decades later, said that he was a disciple of Theodas, a follower of Paul. Scholars do not reject these claims—there is, of course, no way to disprove them—rather, they shrug off the implications by saying that undoubtedly many followers of the apostles misunderstood what they had to say. That is surely true but one must ask: *which* followers?

V

What did the Gnostics write about Jesus? They appear to have been principally interested in recording his "secret" teaching and often he is represented as giving this to select disciples after the resurrection. The *Gospel of Thomas*, to which we have already referred, contains a series of sayings without any connecting narrative. The *Gospel of Philip*, also found at Nag Hammadi in 1946, is a collection of lengthy discourses lacking, again, any clear connecting link. The *Gospel of Truth*, another volume of the Nag Hammadi library, probably the work of Valentinus himself, is an extended homily with one relatively brief account of the life of Jesus. Other

Gnostic works such as the *Apocryphon of John*, the *Pistis Sophia*, the Book of *Thomas the Athlete* are all concerned with more or less esoteric teaching. On the face of it, consequently, the Gnostics seem not to have been interested in what Jesus *did* or what happened to him. But this is more apparent than real. We do not have a Gnostic Gospel which reads like the four canonical ones with which we are familiar, but does that mean none existed? It would be very strange if that were true, not only because, as I hope to show, enough Gnostic or semi-Gnostic material of the traditional gospel type exists, but also, and perhaps chiefly, because, as this same material proves, the Gnostic had his own *version* of what actually did take place.

Where do we find this material? Some of it has been around for thousands of years, by which I mean *known* for all that time; I include in this category the *Acts of John* which I consider to be of very great importance, and the fragments of the *Gospel of the Egyptians*. Some of it was well known for a time and then disappeared; this is true of everything else used, but not all of it reappeared at the same time. A few years before the French Revolution the authorities of the British Museum bought a Coptic manuscript of a work called the *Pistis Sophia* ("Faithful Wisdom") from a London physician. How this gentleman acquired the manuscript is not known. In it, however, are contained selections from a collection of hymns called by the author of the Pistis Sophia, *Odes of Solomon*. More than a century later what appears to be the complete collection of these *Odes* was published by J. Rendell

Harris. Harris, a renowned scholar, had acquired—again we do not know how—a manuscript in which these *Odes* were written out in Syriac, the language of their origin according to the best modern scholarship. Ever since then there has been much discussion as to the kind of milieu from which they emerged and the time of their emergence. It cannot be far from the mark to say that they are very early, probably bordering on the end of the first and the beginning of the second century, and that they come from a Syriac Christian community with some special kind of relationship to the Fourth Gospel. Although the *Odes* show no interest in the cosmological preoccupations of full-blown Gnosticism, their Christology—which concerns us—is decidedly *docetic*. (The human nature of Jesus is not "human" in the way ours is.)

The *Acts of John*, as mentioned above, have been around for a long time, and they were evidently widely read, so much so that when the orthodox Church was in a position to control the ebb and flow of Christian literature, a serious attempt was made to bury these *Acts* and to replace them with a "safer" version which came to be known as the *Acts of Prochorus*. The original *Acts of John* were still in circulation in the tenth century when they were read by Photius, the celebrated diplomat and patriarch of Constantinople. Photius tells us they were written by a certain Leucius Charinus, and Epiphanius (fourth century), no friend of "heretics," tells us that John the evangelist had a disciple named Leucius (which is what the author of the *Acts* claims to be). Certainly these *Acts*, or parts of them at least, were very early (specifically the parts about Jesus) because they were known to Clement of Alexandria in the second century. They deserve much more attention than they are usually given.

Little more than a decade ago Professor Morton Smith of Columbia University discovered part of a long and long-lost letter of Clement of Alexandria to a certain Theodore. The content of this letter is of special interest on two counts; first because it provides new information about an important Gnostic sect, the Carpocratians, who were active in Egypt during the second century, and secondly because it quotes, at some length, from what Clement calls a "secret gospel of Mark." Innumerable questions arise from this discovery which are beyond our special concern, but the fact that it includes a section of a gospel which resembles both the canonical type (narrative with a miracle story) and the Gnostic type (by introducing Salome, the favorite female interlocutress in Gnostic literature), gives it a particular importance to the quest for a *bona fide* Gnostic Gospel. If we were ever to be so fortunate as to unearth the rest of this secret gospel we would probably find that it bears a very close resemblance to the reconstructed gospel attempted here.

We also have part of a *Gospel of Mary* which turned up at the end of the last century and which is thought to derive from the second century. Unfortunately it lacks several pages so that we are not able to reconstruct the content of the teaching, but what does remain is very suggestive of the kind of situation we must assume existed at a time when different Christian groups, some Gnostic, some not, were beginning to wonder whether they could all place themselves under the umbrella of Christianity. The "Mary" of this gospel, by the way, is Mary Magdalene who rather takes the role usually assigned to John as the disciple most loved by Jesus.

By far the most interesting discovery of Gnostic material, however, is that made at Nag Hammadi in Egypt nearly thirty years ago.

I suppose one might say that so many of the most important archaeological discoveries of modern times have been made not by the learned who know what they are looking for, but by the unlettered who do not know what they have found. The Rosetta Stone, found by Napoleonic soldiers in Egypt in 1799, proved to be the key which opened the door to a knowledge of the ancient hieroglyphic script of the pharaohs, something no one had been able to read for fifteen hundred years. In 1887 a peasant woman rummaging around the debris of a city whose very existence had been forgotten for more than three thousand years came upon the archives of one of Egypt's most interesting rulers, the so-called "heretic" pharaoh Ikhnaton, and this correspondence shed enormous light on the history of Palestine in the second millennium B.C. In 1947 an Arab shepherd who went off in search of a missing goat came upon some caves overlooking the Dead Sea in which were stored the many and varied documents we know as the Dead Sea Scrolls. Just a year before, in 1946, some Egyptian *fellahin* in search of manure uncovered another library in a cemetery that had not been used in sixteen hundred years. It has been said that the peasants, totally un-aware of the significance of the ancient papyri, used some of them for kindling in order to brew their tea. Those that survived, and they are numerous, constitute the Nag Hammadi (or Chenoboskion) library (after the site, some sixty miles distant from Luxor, where they were found).

Most of the fifty-odd works included in this veritable treasure trove are Gnostic, but not all are. In fact it is difficult to say what purpose this library served. Near Nag Hammadi are the remains of a great Christian monastery founded by St. Pachomius at about the same time this library was buried; but it was certainly not buried by the monks, who would have burned it. The usual assumption is that it belonged to some Gnostic community which quit the area with the arrival of the formidable Pachomius, but there is good reason to think that the manuscripts were collected by a scribe for some wealthy customer interested in esoterica. One of the texts bears a curious little note by the scribe telling his patron that he assumes he has already received or purchased copies of the remaining volumes of the series and adding that he did not want to bore his employer with material he had already read—hardly a reaction he would have anticipated in his patron if the latter were a *dévot*. For some reason the scribe must have found it necessary to leave the area in haste (perhaps one of the monks learned that someone in the area had a collection of heretical literature) but expected to return and deposited his manuscripts in a pagan cemetery, not a likely place for monks to frequent.

Whatever the explanation, the mysterious burial of these documents was most fortuitous for us. We now have a considerable amount of Gnostic material where previously we had only fragments and summaries provided by the early Church Fathers like Irenaeus, Hippolytus, and Epiphanius for apologetic and polemical purposes. From this Gnostic library we have selected here excerpts from the three so-called gospels, that of Thomas, that of Philip, and the *Gospel of Truth*.

VI

Does it matter that we dare to say we have recovered a Gnostic Jesus? For those to whom Jesus is a unique religious figure anything we learn about him is of interest, howsoever different or unlikely. But I venture to say that this is more than an exercise in curiosity. The Jesus of "orthodoxy" appeals to all those who believe that the world is essentially good, an object of deep concern to its creator. The evil that exists is the result of human greed, but man, as such, is indefinitely perfectible, capable of overcoming his shortcomings and destined to transform this world into a restored paradise. This view is implicit—and that is really too weak a word—in the Old Testament, and, though it was for centuries tempered by the Christian doctrine of Original Sin, it has re-emerged in what is generally recognized as the "new" theology (which interprets Original Sin as a social influence). The religious dialogue in the contemporary Western world—and perhaps in the East as well—is all about social and economic reform, political justice and political revolution, and, above all, community. All of this assumes that man is capable of transforming his world, presumably for the better. And all of this can be said and done in the name of Christianity because the ethical concerns of the Old Testament are strongly represented in the New.

But there are many other thinkers in today's world who view it as a bad joke. They will point to the fact, first of all, that no social revolution has ever succeeded because the rabid revolutionaries soon turn out, when successful, to be a new establishment imposing the same kinds of discrimination under a new banner. Even if an ultimately viable Utopia were to be established, what, they want to know, is to prevent the kinds of devastating misery caused by floods, droughts, earthquakes, volcanic eruptions, and all their consequences? Is man destined to master these vagaries of Nature? Let us say that he will; what then will he do when our sun either turns to ice or explodes into a nova burning everything in the solar system to a crisp? Will we as a race by then have made the great voyage to other galaxies? That is not inconceivable, but according to the law of entropy no place in our immeasurably vast universe is spared the ultimate fate of cosmic death. In such a view, and it is, though pessimistic, realistic, the material world seems indeed to be a bad joke.

In thinking along these lines the modern atheist existentialist comes very close to the Gnostic perspective. The Gnostic differed from him in one important respect: he believed that there was something in man, though not necessarily in all men, which, in a very literal sense, belonged to another world, a world beyond matter and its decay. To accept this—and he accepted it because he felt that his ability to recognize the world as a terrible mistake was an unmistakable sign that he did not really belong to it—was to accept hope. Not hope that things would get better but hope that he was not *just* a part of the mistake, and that somehow he would regain that world beyond matter from which he ultimately derived.

As we noted at the beginning there are as many projections of Jesus today as there are fertile imaginations. The Jesus of the Gnostics will necessarily strike most readers as another kind of caricature. In most respects, he certainly is, but both because Gnosticism was in circulation at so early a date and because it represents a philosophy which has found favor again at this late date, it has a claim on our attention.

The Gospel Text

I have imposed my own style on the translated materials so as to facilitate the reading of the constructed text, and my rendering is often free though never unfaithful. There are various translations into English of the texts used but my own competence in the relevant ancient languages has not obliged me to depend upon them. Sections in italic are those from the four Gospels of the Bible that are discussed in the introduction and fit well in this Gnostic context.

Conception and Birth

The Holy Spirit bared her bosom and mixed the milk of the breasts of the Father. This was the milk which the womb of the virgin received and she conceived and gave birth. She became a mother, though a virgin, and though she labored in bringing forth the Son, she had no pain; neither did she require a midwife for what happened was designed and he who was born enabled her to give life.

The Odes of Solomon 19.

Baptism

Now the mother of Jesus and his brothers said to him: "There is John who baptizes for the remission of sins; let us go and be baptized by him." And Jesus said: "What is the sin that I have committed, or how have I been overcome by evil?" But then he said: "Perhaps what I have just said is a sin of ignorance." [And they went to be baptized] and when he was being baptized a brilliant light shimmered over the water so that all who had come there were afraid. A dove fluttered above the head of Jesus and sang, and all heard the voice of the dove and all, again, were afraid, both those who came from nearby and those who came from afar. And Jesus said: "I seem to them like a stranger because I am from another race." And again he said: *"Truly, I say to you, among those born of women there has risen no one greater than John the Baptist; yet he who is least in the kingdom of heaven is greater than he. From the days of John the Baptist until now the kingdom of heaven has suffered violence and men of violence take it by force. For all the prophets and the Law prophesied until John."* "I have come," he said, "to make the things below like the things above and the external like the internal and I have come to make them all one in this very place."

The Gospel of the Hebrews: Fragment; The Gospel of Thomas: Saying 104; Matthew: Codex Vercellensis, Codex Sangermanensis; The Odes of Solomon 24 and 41; Matthew 11:11–13; The Gospel of Philip (69).

The Beginning of the Public Ministry

He became a guide; he was tranquil and he was unhurried. He came as into the midst of a school and he spoke the word like a master. There came to him those who, in their own estimation, were wise; they tested him but he confounded them because they were empty people and they hated him because they were not truly men of heart. And Jesus said: "I came into the midst of the world and in the flesh was I seen by them but I found them all intoxicated, yet not one was athirst and my soul strives for the sons of men because they are blind and see not with their hearts." And after these there came to him the little children, those who possess the knowledge of the Father. And he said: *"The kingdom of heaven may be compared to a man who sowed good seed in his field; but while men were sleeping, his enemy* came and sowed weeds among the wheat, and went away. So when the plants came up and bore grain, then the weeds appeared also. And the servants of the householder came and said to him, 'Sir, did you not sow good seed in your field? How then has it weeds?' He said to them, 'An enemy has done this.' The servants said to him, 'Then do you want us to go and gather them?' But he said, 'No, lest in gathering the weeds you root up the wheat along with them.' "

The Gospel of Truth; The Gospel of Thomas: Saying 28; Matthew 13:24–29.

The Special Election of John

John, the son of Zebedee, saw Jesus as a young man. John was about to be married but Jesus came to him and said: "I have need of you." And John became ill and was compelled to postpone the marriage. Twice again the marriage day was fixed but John lost his sight and remained in that state for two years until, finally, he saw Jesus again on the seashore.

Acts of John (113).

The Call of the First Disciples

While he was at the Sea of Galilee Jesus chose Peter and Andrew, who were brothers, as disciples. And he came upon John and James, who were also brothers, and he said to them: "I have need of you, come follow me." James, hearing him, said to his brother John: "What does this child on the seashore

who has called to us want?" And John said: "What
child?" To which James replied: "The very one
who calls us." And John said: "We have been a
long time at sea James, and I am afraid your vision
is blurred. Is not the man you see handsome, fair, and
cheerful?" But James replied: "I see no such man,
brother, but let us go and find out what this person
wants." They went to shore much perplexed,
wondering what it was that they had seen so differently and what it meant. Then Jesus entered the
house of Levi who was a dyer and he took seventy-
two cloths of different colors and threw them all
into the vat and when he took them out they were
all white and he said: "The Son of man, as you see,
comes as a dyer." And Jesus said: "I shall choose
you, one out of a thousand and two out of ten
thousand, and you shall be as a single one." And
again he said: "*The kingdom of heaven may be
compared to a king who gave a marriage feast for
his son. . . . But when the king came in to look at
the guests he saw there a man who had no wedding
garment; and he said to him, 'Friend, how did you
get in here without a wedding garment?' And he
was speechless. Then the king said to the attendants,
bind him hand and foot and cast him into the outer
darkness; there men will weep and gnash their teeth.'
For many are called, but few are chosen.*" Then
Jesus said: "If they ask you where you have come
from, tell them, 'We have come from the Light.' "

*Acts of John (88–89); The Gospel of Philip (54); The
Gospel of Thomas: Sayings 23 and 50; Matthew 22:2, 11–14.*

Conflict with a Chief Priest

Jesus took his disciples into the Temple enclosure, into the place of holiness itself, and a chief priest, who was a Pharisee and whose name was Levi, accosted them and said to Jesus: "Who has given you permission to walk about in here and to gaze upon these sacred vessels without having bathed yourself, and without your disciples having even washed their feet?" Jesus stood his ground and said to him: "Well, now, how much better off are you? Are you clean?" The priest answered: "Of course I am, for I have washed in the pool of David and I have donned clean white garments and only then did I come here to regard these holy things." Whereupon Jesus said to him: "You poor blind men who see nothing. You have washed yourself in water that flows and in which dogs and pigs wallow day and night, and you scrub your skin which whores also do, and it is the skin which the flute girls anoint with perfume and beautify in order to arouse lust in men but, as we know, their hearts are full of scorpions and base intent. I, and my disciples, on the other hand, whom you say are unclean, have bathed in the living water which descends from the Father in Heaven." Then Jesus said to the disciples: *"Every plant which my heavenly Father has not planted will be rooted up. Let them alone; they are blind guides. And if a blind man leads a blind man, both will fall into a pit."* [And since Jesus had spoken so lightly about the teaching of the Pharisees] his disciples said to him: "Is circumcision necessary or not?" And he an-

swered: "If it were necessary then every father
would beget a circumcised male from his mother."

*Oxyrynchus Papyrus V, 840; Matthew 15:13–14; The Gospel
of Thomas: Saying 53.*

The Miracle of the Loaves

And Jesus and his disciples were invited by a
Pharisee to dinner, and they accepted the invitation.
And before each of them, Jesus included, the host
set a loaf. Jesus broke the loaf that had been given
him, and he blessed it and he distributed it to his
disciples; and of the little that each one of them had
received each was filled and they took nothing of
their own loaves. On seeing this the host and his
associates were truly amazed. And Jesus said to his
disciples: "If the flesh is a result of the spirit it is re-
markable, but if the spirit exists for the body it is
mind-boggling and I marvel at how such treasure
can find a home in such poverty."

Acts of John (93); The Gospel of Thomas: Saying 29.

Raising a Dead Man and Conversation
on Life, Death, and Women

Jesus and his disciples came to Bethany where a
certain woman, whose brother had died, came before
Jesus and prostrating herself begged: "Son of David,
have mercy on me." The disciples tried to turn her
away but Jesus, provoked, went with her into the
garden where the tomb was, and a loud cry issued
from the tomb. Jesus, going immediately to the
tomb, and rolling away the stone, stretched forth

his hand over the youth and raised him up, taking him by the hand. When the youth looked at Jesus he loved him, and begged that he might remain with him. When they left the tomb they went into the house of the youth, for the young man was wealthy. Jesus stayed there six days and on the last evening, having given the young man instructions, the youth came to him in the evening wearing nothing but a linen cloth, and he stayed that night while Jesus taught him the mystery of the kingdom of God. The next day Jesus returned to the other side of the Jordan and came to Jericho where he found the sister of the young man whom Jesus had raised and loved, and the young man's mother and Salome, but Jesus did not wish to speak to them. Thereupon Salome said: "Who are you, sir, and whose son? You took your ease on my couch and ate from my table." Jesus said to her: "I am He who is from the Uniform and the things of the Father have been given to me." Salome said: "But I am your disciple." Jesus answered: "Well, then, if (the disciple) is one [with the Father] he will be filled with light, but if he is divided, he will be filled with darkness." Salome said again: "For how long shall men continue to die?" Jesus said: "As long as you women bear children." Salome responded: "Then I have done well in having no children." Jesus said: "Eat all plants save those which are bitter. I came to destroy the works of the female." At this point Peter said to Jesus: "Let Mary (Magdalene) leave our company because women are not worthy of the true Life." But Jesus answered him saying: "Watch, I shall lead her so that I will make her into a male and she too will then become a living spirit like the rest of you; for every woman who makes herself male will enter the kingdom of heaven." Then all the disciples said to him: "Why do you love Mary (Magdalene) more than us?" Jesus replied: "Why do you suppose I do not love you as much as her?"

The Letter of Clement of Alexandria to Theodore; The Gospel of Thomas: Saying 61; The Gospel According to the Egyptians: Fragments; The Gospel of Thomas: Saying 114; The Gospel of Philip (55).

Conversation with the Disciples

The disciples said to Jesus: "We know that you are about to leave us; who is it that will then take first place among us?" Jesus said to them: "Wherever you may find yourselves you will go to James the Just on account of whom heaven and earth came into being." Then Jesus asked them: "Tell me whom I am like." Simon Peter said to him: "You are like a faultless angel." Matthew said: "You are like a philosopher, full of wisdom." Thomas said to him: "Master, I am speechless when it comes to describing you." Jesus said: "I am not your Master; you have drunk deeply from the spring I have measured out and hence you speak like a drunkard." Then he took Thomas aside and spoke three words to him. When Thomas rejoined his companions they asked him what Jesus had said to him. He replied: "If I tell you one of the words he uttered to me you will stone me and fire will come from the stones and consume you." Then the disciples said to Jesus: "Who are you that you should say such things to us?" Jesus answered them: "From what I say to you you fail to understand who I am, rather, you have become like the Jews for they admire the tree but dislike its fruit and they cherish the fruit but detest the tree." And again he said: *"To what shall I compare this generation? It is like children sitting in the market places and calling to their playmates, 'We piped to you, and you did not dance; we wailed and you did not mourn.' For John came neither eating nor drinking, and they say, 'he has a demon'; the Son of man came eating and drinking, and they say, 'Behold, a glutton and a drunkard, a friend of tax collectors and sinners!' Yet Sophia is justified by her children."*

The Gospel of Thomas: Sayings 12–13 and 43; Matthew 11:16–19.

The Action of Judas Iscariot

And the chief priests and Pharisees were of a mind to apprehend Jesus for they saw that if they left him alone all would believe in him. But they were afraid to seize him because of the multitude and because the Passover was near at hand. Many Jews came up to Jerusalem for the Passover. Judas Iscariot said to Jesus secretly: "Is it not true Lord that the whole world lies in the power of the Evil One and that the things above and the things below must be dissolved?" And Jesus answered him: "So it is, Judas; *how can one enter a strong man's house and plunder his goods, unless he first binds the strong man? Then indeed he may plunder his house.* When I am lifted up, in that hour will the Prince of this World be cast out in chains." And Judas said to him: "See how the chief priests and Pharisees are afraid to touch you. Are they not thus delaying the hour of dissolution?" Jesus said to him: "What you must do, do quickly." And Judas went forth and told the chief priests how they might seize Jesus secretly by night, without fear of the people. But the other disciples did not know that Jesus had commissioned Judas to deliver him into the hands of his enemies.

Free reconstruction from fragments preserved by Irenaeus, Tertullian, and Epiphanius and from Matthew 12:29.

The Last Supper

Before he was about to be arrested by the lawless Jews—they who had their Law from the lawless serpent who is the devil—Jesus gathered all the disciples together; and as he was about to ask for the bread and the cup and bless them, Mary (Magdalene) laughed, so Jesus asked that the women leave. Then he said to the disciples: "Before I am delivered up let us sing a hymn to the Father and then go forth to whatever awaits us." He said to them: "Form a circle, holding one another's hands, and I will stand in the middle. After each verse that I sing, answer 'Amen.'" And so he began to sing the hymn and they, moving around in the circle, responded "Amen."

Glory be to thee, Father; Glory be to thee, O Word; Glory be to thee Grace. Amen. Glory be to thee, the Spirit; Glory be to thee, O Holy One; Glory be to the Glory which is yours. Amen.

We praise thee, O Father; we give thanks to thee,
   Light in which no darkness dwells. Amen.
I tell you why we give thanks:
I wish to be saved, and I wish to save. Amen.
I wish to be freed, and I wish to free. Amen.
I wish to be broken, and I wish to break. Amen.
I wish to be born, and I wish to give birth. Amen.
I wish to eat, and I wish to be consumed. Amen.
I wish to hear, and I wish to be heard. Amen.
I wish to be understood being, myself, total Mind.
I wish to wash myself, and I wish to wash. Amen.

Grace is dancing
I wish to play the flute; all of you dance. Amen.
I wish to sing a dirge; all of you beat your breasts.
   Amen.
The number Eight sings praises along with us. Amen.
The number Twelve dances on high. Amen.
I wish to adorn, and I wish adornments. Amen.
I wish to be united, and I wish to unite. Amen.
I have no house; yet I have houses. Amen.
I have no place; yet I have places. Amen.
I have no shrine; yet I have shrines. Amen.
I am a lamp to you who see me. Amen.
I am a mirror to you who know me. Amen.
I am a door to you who knock upon me. Amen.
I am a way to you the wayfarer. Amen.

Now respond to my dancing; behold yourself in
me who speak, and, seeing what I do, say nothing of
my mysteries. Do you who dance understand what I
do, for this passion of manhood I am about to suffer
is yours. You could not at all have understood what
you suffer if I had not been sent to you as the word
of the Father.

You have me as a bed; rest upon me. Who I am you shall know when I depart; what I am now seen to be I am not. Whenever you come you will see.

The disciples then said to him: "Tell us how our end will be." Jesus said: "Have you then discovered the beginning so that you can ask about the end? Where the beginning is, there also shall be the end. Blessed is he who shall stand at the beginning and he shall know the end and he shall not taste death."

Acts of John (94–96); Apostolic Church Order; The Gospel of Thomas: Saying 18.

Crucifixion and Appearance to John

Having danced with them the Lord went forth and the disciples, like men lost or groggy with sleep, fled this way and that. Not even John, when he saw him suffer, stayed by his side but fled to a cave on the Mount of Olives and there he wept. And when Jesus was crucified, at the sixth hour, a darkness covered the earth. But the Lord, standing in the midst of the cave lighted it up and said: "John, in the eyes of the crowd below in Jerusalem I am being crucified and pierced with lances and reeds, and I am being given gall and vinegar to drink but nothing of the things which they will say of me have I suffered; the suffering which I disclosed to you and to the others in the dance, that I would have called a mystery. What you are you perceive because I showed it to you, but what I am I alone know and no other man."

Acts of John (97, 101).

44

Ascension and Going Forth of the Apostles

[And Jesus appeared to the disciples and said:] "Go therefore and preach the gospel of the kingdom; *Do not give dogs what is holy; and do not throw your pearls before swine, lest they trample them under foot and turn to attack you.* I have left no commandment but what I have commanded you and I have given you no Law, as did the lawgiver, for I would not have you bound by it."

When he said this he went away. But the disciples were very sad and mourned at length saying: "How shall we go to the Gentiles and preach the gospel of the kingdom of the Son of man? For if even he was not spared suffering how shall we escape it?

Then Mary (Magdalene) stood up and after a greeting said to her brother disciples: "Do not lament or be sorrowful or weak, for his grace will be with you all and will be as a shield. Instead, let us praise his greatness, for he formed us and made us into men." After Mary had spoken the disciples were encouraged and they began to talk about the things Jesus had said. Peter said to Mary: "Sister, we know that the Savior loved you more than other women. Let us hear from you those words of his which you have in mind which we have not heard but which you know." Mary answered and said: "What is hidden from you I will disclose." And she began (. . . to talk about the soul, many words, and then she said that the soul knows) "that all will go free, things both earthly and heavenly" (. . . and that the soul rises upward against seven powers of wrath . . .) They ask the soul: "Whence do you come, man-killer, or where are you going, conqueror of space?" The soul answers and says: "Whatever seizes me is killed and what turns me about is overthrown; my desire has reached an end and ignorance is dead. I, a world, I was saved from a world and from the chains of the impotence of knowledge, the existence of which is tied to time. From now on I shall reach rest in the time of the moment of Eternity in silence."

When Mary had said these things she kept silence for the Savior had said just so much to her. But Andrew spoke up and said: "Say what you think concerning what she said, for I do not believe that the Lord spoke in this way. These teachings seem clearly to be different from his." Peter also opposed her in regard to these statements and turning to the disciples he queried: "Did he then speak secretly with a woman in preference to us? Are we to reconsider and listen to her? Did he prefer her to us?" At which Mary grieved and said to Peter: "My brother, can you think that I made all this up and that I am lying concerning the Savior?" Levi spoke now and said to Peter: "Peter you are always irate. Here you are battling with this woman as though she were an adversary. If the Savior made her worthy, who are you to discredit her? Surely the Savior knew her very well and he loved her more than he loved us. Should we not rather be ashamed and put on the Perfect Man as he commanded, and proclaim the gospel and leave aside further commandments or further law?" When Levi said this they began to go out in order to proclaim and preach the Savior.

The Gospel of Mary; Matthew 7:6.

Evangelist's Epilogue

They nailed him to a tree;
He affixed the testamentary disposition
of the Father
to the Cross.
Oh the greatness of such teaching!
He brings himself downward to death
while eternal life clothes him;
He divested himself of these rags which perish;
He clothes himself with imperishability
which no one has the power to take from him.

The Gospel of Truth.

𝒩otes

Conception and Birth

These lines are excerpted from the *Odes of Solomon* (Ode 19:4–9). Scholarly opinion has long been divided on the question of whether or not these *Odes* are Gnostic. J. H. Charlesworth, one of the foremost contemporary authorities on the *Odes*, argues that they are not Gnostic, but he admits that they are "a tributary to Gnosticism." R. M. Grant, Hans Jonas, K. Rudolph, R. Bultmann and other students of Gnosticism are convinced of the Gnostic provenance of these odes. We can safely characterize them as "semi-Gnostic." The date of the *Odes* has also been disputed. Charlesworth assigns a first century date to them and locates them in the same milieu which gave birth to the Gospel of John. Charlesworth has edited the latest critical edition of the *Odes* (Oxford, 1973) and has contributed two valuable articles to the ongoing discussion: "The Odes of Solomon—Not Gnostic" *Catholic Biblical Quarterly* 31 (1969): 357–369; "The Odes of Solomon and the Gospel of John" *CBQ* 35 (1973): 298–322.

This excerpt, given the very early date of the *Odes*, must be ranked with the prologues of Matthew, Luke, and John. The language in the first two lines is highly metaphorical and strange-sounding to us. Here, and elsewhere in the *Odes*, the Holy Spirit is feminine, reflecting a Semitic background (in Hebrew and Aramaic "Spirit" is feminine; in Syriac, in which these *Odes* are written, it is usually masculine, but not so here), yet it is the Father whose breasts are milked. Unlike Matthew and Luke the stress here is not on the unusual events surrounding the conception of Jesus but on the circumstances of his birth: "without pain," "she did not require a midwife." This is evidence for a very early origin of the belief that the mother of Jesus retained the physical signs of virginity even in childbirth.

In later, fully developed Gnostic literature, little, if any, interest is taken in the conception and birth of Jesus. On the one hand certain Gnostics taught that the Christos—the heavenly emissary—descended upon the man Jesus at the time of his baptism and departed from him at the time of his crucifixion (which means, of course, that neither the birth nor the death of the man Jesus had any significance at all), while, on the other hand, Gnostics like the followers of Ptolemaeus admitted that Christ was born in human fashion and had a real body, but this body was not human, rather it was fashioned of material from the stars and did not come *from* Mary but only passed *through* her. In the ode before us Mary appears to have been the mother of Jesus in the strict sense of the word; she conceived and gave birth, but it is worth noting that in other odes of the series (28:17; 41:8) Jesus speaks of himself as being of "another race" and as one who is *not* the "brother" of men.

Baptism

This excerpt is made up of fragments from the lost *Gospel of the Hebrews* (probably an Egyptian work not distinctively Gnostic but tinged by the pervasive Gnosticism of the Egyptian milieu); the *Gospel of Thomas* (Saying 104); a very ancient variant reading to Matthew 3:16; *Odes of Solomon* 24 and 41; and the *Gospel of Philip* (Saying 69). The reaction of Jesus to the suggestion of his mother and brothers is peculiar. In one sense it has a distinctly Johannine cast: the question "What sin have I committed?" is immediately reminiscent of John 8:46; 14:30; and 1 John 3:5, but the seemingly perplexed reply he gives to his own question has Gnostic overtones. In the view of many Gnostics the man Jesus would have been in ignorance until he received the divine Christos at the time of baptism, and for them ignorance was the only real sin. The concluding statement: "I have come to make the things below . . ." is decidedly Gnostic, affirming that his mission as revealer is to reunite the *Pleroma* and to do it here on the very scene where the scattering and alienation originally took place. The intermediate reference to the fluttering dove is, of course, a parallel to Mark 1:10–11 (*see also* Matt. 3:16–17; Luke 3:21–22; John 1:32) with a difference: it is not the voice of the Father which is heard here but the voice of the dove, i.e., of the Spirit.

The Beginning of the Public Ministry

The first and third excerpts in this section may be found in the *Gospel of Truth*, one of the tractates of the Nag Hammadi library. This gospel is thought by many to be the work of Valentinus, one of the best known Gnostic teachers of the second century. An Egyptian, Valentinus first taught in Alexandria and then moved on to Rome where he gained a following (ca. 135–155). There is almost nothing of the bizarre cosmological speculation common to later Valentinian writings in this work, which is a principal reason for assigning it to Valentinus or one of his early disciples. For an excellent translation and commentary on the *Gospel of Truth* the reader is referred to K. Grobel, *The Gospel of Truth* (London, 1960).

The first and third excerpts given here belong together in the *Gospel of Truth*. They summarize in a general but poetic way the gospel presentation of Jesus as a teacher (notice that there is no reference here to any miracles; for the Gnostic, miracles were, if not demonic, irrelevant) and the hostile reaction to him of the scribes and Pharisees contrasted with the acceptance of him by the humble disciples. Grobel rightly calls attention to the similarity between this passage in the *Gospel of Truth* and Matt. 11:25 (*see also* Luke 10:21): "I thank thee Father . . . that thou hast hidden these things from the wise and understanding and revealed them to babes."

The intermediate excerpt was first known to the scholarly world at the turn of the century, being part of one of the Oxyrhynchus papyri discovered by B. P. Grenfell and A. S. Hunt. These papyri contain sayings of Jesus each of which begins with the statement: "Jesus says." Since then, as a result of the Nag Hammadi finds, we know that these sayings are part of the *Gospel of Thomas*, or that they ultimately became such. The papyri are much earlier (ca. 200) than the *Gospel of Thomas* manuscript. Neither in the latter volume nor in the papyri is any circumstantial background given to the sayings. This one seems appropriate as a sort of initial appraisal by Jesus of the scene he came upon. The first two lines are very "Johannine" in flavor (cp. John 1:9–14: "The true light . . . was coming into the world . . . and the Word became flesh") and the next three quite Gnostic; "drunkenness" is a favorite Gnostic image for the human condition. The last line, once again, is reminiscent of the Fourth Gospel (cp. John 9:40–41). For a commentary on the saying the reader is referred to J. Jeremias, *Unknown Sayings of Jesus* (London, 1958), pp. 69–74.

The Special Election of John

This excerpt is taken from the *Acts of John*, a Gnostic work of the second century attributed to a certain Leucius, whom Epiphanius states was a disciple of the fourth evangelist. The chapters in these *Acts* which deal with the ministry of Jesus (most of the material deals with the travels of John) are of particular interest, not merely because they offer another version of incidents well known from the canonical Gospels but also because they are found in a Gnostic work. They are evidence that a Gnostic *Gospel* in the accepted sense of the term, is not to be precluded. Where I use these Acts in this compilation I have altered the first person pronoun (I or we) to the third. In the *Acts* it is always "John" who speaks. Gnostic sects, as a rule, regarded marriage as a perpetuation of the unhappy cycle of birth and death necessitated by a material creation. The true Gnostic could not, in conscience, wish to bring into this warped world other unhappy souls. In this brief extract John, "the beloved disciple," is preserved by Jesus, even before receiving his call, from entering into marriage. In chapter 2 of the canonical Gospel of John (2:1–11), Jesus attends a marriage which some exegetes have suggested was the marriage of John. This is bald hypothesis but it is not at all impossible that the story there is partly intended as a contradiction to the Gnostic teaching on marriage and legends, such as the one we read here from the *Acts of John*, about the beloved disciple.

The Call of the First Disciples

The first part of this excerpt is taken, again, from the *Acts of John* though it is separated from the passage given above by several paragraphs (which probably accounts for the fact that John, as we meet him here, does not seem to be suffering from any blindness). This account of the call of the first disciples agrees with the synoptic Gospels in locating the event at the sea of Galilee and in naming the first chosen as Andrew and Peter, James and John, but of course the reference to Jesus as someone who appeared differently to different people has no canonical parallel. We do find the idea elsewhere however. In the *Acts of Peter* another, slightly later second century document, the apostle says: "For each one of us could only see him (Jesus) as he was able, according to his capacity for seeing." The early second century Gnostic Basilides maintained that the Christ, being a *virtus incorporalis* (a bodiless power), could transform himself at will and at will make himself invisible. It may well be that Basilides and these other writings are all influenced by Buddhist literature. In the *Mahaparinibbana-sutta* (III, 21–23) the Buddha says that there are many kinds of assemblies and that as he enters each assembly he makes himself look like the other members of the group and makes his voice like theirs. A little further on in this same section from the *Acts of John* the apostle says: "And frequently when I walked with him, I wanted to see the print of his foot, whether it appeared on the earth; for I saw him, as it were, lifting himself up from the earth; and I never did see [the footprint]." This too has parallels in Buddhist legend according to which the Buddha never touched the ground: "The plant of his feet is not stained by dust." Others see in this a more ancient Egyptian influence. For a more detailed study of these interesting Buddhist-Christian parallels and the possibility of Buddhist influence on early Christian Docetism and Gnosticism the reader is referred to H. de Lubac: *Aspects of Buddhism* (New York, 1954; esp. chap. 3, "Different Manifestations of Christ and the Buddha").

The episode relating to the dying of cloths (corresponding to the call of Levi in Mark 2:14) comes from the *Gospel of Philip* (54) and is a variation on the theme expressed at the end of the baptism account. The final statements both come from the *Gospel of Thomas* and obviously suit the context of election.

Conflict with a Chief Priest

This otherwise unknown story about an encounter between Jesus and Levi the priest is all that remains of a tiny parchment gospel-book discovered on the same site as the Oxyrhynchus papyri mentioned earlier. Jeremias (*Unknown Sayings of Jesus*, pp. 36–49) discusses it at length and believes it to be authentic. The story has a number of parallels with Mark 7:1–8, but the conclusion to which it leads is more Johannine than synoptic, recalling such texts as John 3:5–6; 4:14; 7:37–

39. Moreover the conclusion reads suspiciously like a Gnostic allusion to the fact that Jesus, no less than his disciples, has received the gift of Gnosis (here described as living water) from the Father, which distinguishes him (and them) from "ye blind that see not" who are concerned with the ineffective externals of the Law.

I have concluded the episode with another question and answer from the *Gospel of Thomas* because it echoes Jesus' disdain for the Law as the Gnostics portrayed it. Circumcision was, for the Jew, the basic sign of adherence to the covenant with Yahweh. Paul too discounted the material efficacy of circumcision (e.g., Gal. 3:6: "For in Christ Jesus neither circumcision nor uncircumcision is of any avail") but the words of Jesus here are much stronger and actually flippant.

The Miracle of the Loaves

This excerpt is taken from the *Acts of John* (93) already discussed. What we have here is obviously a parallel to the canonical accounts of Jesus' multiplication of the loaves but with striking differences. Jesus does not here multiply anything and those fed on the one loaf are not four or five thousand (Mark 6, 34–44; 8:1–9, 19–20) but the twelve disciples. Yet as in the canonical accounts all are satisfied and twelve loaves (twelve baskets full in the Fourth Gospel) are saved. The miracle here is in the ability of the disciples to be nourished on so little.

A comparison with something said of Jesus by Valentinus (in one of the few extant genuine fragments of his writings) is inevitable: Jesus, he says, "ate and drank in a peculiar manner, not evacuating his food. So much power of continence was in him that in him food was not corrupted, since he himself had no corruptibility." G. R. S. Mead comments on this: "The 'power' described above by Valentinus is one of the *siddhis* mentioned in every treatise on *yoga* in India, and in the Upanishads we read that 'very little waste' is one of the first signs of 'success in yoga.' " Mastery of this power leads to the eventual substitution of a body of a higher form of matter. Mead thinks that ideas like these lie behind the Docetism of Valentinus and other early Christian Gnostics (cp. *Fragments of a Faith Forgotten* [New Hyde Park, N.Y.: 1960], p. 302). We have already seen that in the account of the Call of the Disciples the author of these *Acts of John* appears to reflect certain Buddhist notions; here we seem to have another example of Indian influence.

I have added here another saying from the *Gospel of Thomas* which is best appreciated in this particular context for Jesus is, in effect, denigrating man's physical envelope and marveling that the soul can even exist in a body.

Raising a Dead Man and Conversation on Life, Death, and Women

This excerpt is taken from a letter of Clement of Alexandria which was unknown until discovered by Morton Smith of Columbia University in the library of Mar Saba Monastery, Jerusalem, in 1958. The letter, which is unfortunately incomplete, was addressed to a certain Theodore and deals with the teachings of a Gnostic sect known as the Carpocratians. The latter, it seems, made use of a "secret gospel of Mark" and Theodore is curious to know more about it. Clement admits that such a gospel exists and that it was indeed the work of Mark the evangelist though "a more spiritual gospel for the use of those who were being perfected." Clement then quotes the passage reproduced here, evidently because in the version of it known to Theodore, it contained the phrase "naked man with naked man" which Clement asserts is not part of the original text. It is a pity that we know nothing more about this "secret gospel." The fact that Clement thought it was authentically Marcan is no guarantee;

the great Alexandrian writer was not very critical in his judgment of pseudocanonical literature. There are good reasons for thinking this "secret gospel" originated in Gnostic circles; not just the fact that the Carpocratians used it (the Gnostics were the first to use the Gospel of John) but especially the introduction into the text of Salome who is a kind of Gnostic interlocutress in so much of their literature. Then too, even though Clement says the phrase "naked man with naked man" does not appear in the original text, there is something peculiar about the detail of the youth coming to Jesus with a linen cloth over his naked body and remaining the night; indeed Professor Smith has constructed an elaborate theory about the actual practices of Jesus on the basis of this (*see* his *The Secret Gospel* [New York, 1973]). The Carpocratians and some other Gnostics reportedly practiced homosexual acts and this detail in the "secret gospel" *suggests*, at least, that for them Jesus did also.

Apart from these observations we have to note that the story is an interesting variant of the raising of Lazarus in John 11 and is sure to assist scholars in their attempts to uncover the source material of the Fourth Gospel.

The excerpts which follow the narrative in this section are taken, respectively, from the *Gospel of Thomas* and the *Gospel of the Egyptians* (known to us chiefly through extracts preserved in the writings of Clement of Alexandria) and the *Gospel of Philip*. I have introduced them here because the first one seems entirely appropriate as Salome's reaction to the fact that Jesus would not receive her (in the Letter of Clement excerpt). The second also follows logically upon a miracle of raising a dead man. The first words to Salome are somewhat enigmatic; who is the "he" who, "if he is the Same" will be filled with light, etc.? Surely not God. A disciple? In that case we have authentic Gnostic teaching here: the disciple who is "the Same," i.e., who knows himself to be one with the Father in nature, will be filled with light; but if the disciple is divided (a *psychic* or *hylic* in Gnostic terminology), then he will be filled with darkness. The statements in the second selection are clearly Gnostic. For Gnostics the material world is evil, the product of ignorant creatures of Sophia. The human body is man's prison and the cause of our ignorance about the true Father. When Jesus says that he has come to destroy the works of the female he means, especially, the consequences of being born in a body of flesh. It is another way of saying "I have come to bring Gnosis (knowledge)" because Gnosis cancels out the effects of being born of flesh and blood.

When taken at face value the words of the Gnostic Jesus appear excessively harsh and anti-feminist, but Salome and Mary Magdalene (who is introduced in the final excerpt of this section) play an important part in Gnostic literature. In fact, as we shall see, the Magdalene sometimes assumes the role of the most loved disciple (something clearly hinted at here), the person to whom Jesus confides especially important revelations. The individual woman is not inferior to the individual man since either may be a psychic, either a hylic, but woman has the additional shame of bearing and bringing forth new victims of the primordial mistake. Jesus, as we see here, is destined to make women men, free them, that is, from their physiological role in order to lift them to contemplation. Nevertheless, even the Gnostic, who theoretically viewed any and all sexuality as alien to the Father's world and will, is affected by the low opinion of woman which was part of the cultural scene of antiquity. We see this in the characterization of that member of the Pleroma who "fell from Grace"—Sophia—as female. This is part of the general conviction that the female is weaker than the male; Peter is the spokesman here for this point of view, but notice that Jesus counters the assertion that women "are not worthy of the True Life" by saying that he will make the Magdalene "like the rest of you." This was the Gnostic charter for "equal opportunities for women."

Conversation with the Disciples

The first and longer excerpt here is taken from the newly discovered *Gospel of Thomas* to which frequent reference has already been made. This passage is of great interest because it parallels Mark 8:27–30; Matthew 16:13–16; Luke 9:18–21; and John 6:67–69. At the same time it is very distinctive. In the synoptics the incident is located at Caesarea Philippi and in all four canonical accounts only Peter is singled out by name. In the synoptics, again, the "disciples," generally, reply: "John the Baptist, and others say Elijah and others (Jeremiah or) one of the prophets." As we see, the answers given here are quite different. Simon Peter's reply is quite interesting: "Thou art like a righteous angel." "Angel" in Greek and Hebrew means "messenger." This is what the heavenly revealer is, essentially, in Gnostic liter-ture: a messenger from above. The answer of Matthew seems rather prosaic—"a wise man of understanding"— but it is really very significant in terms of how the Gospel of Matthew presents Jesus; he is, there, above all a teacher and a teacher of wisdom; he is not only a wise man but Wisdom incarnate (cp. Matt. 11:16–30; 12:42). We are to suppose that Thomas has caught the "essence" of Jesus because he confesses to an unut-terable understanding. Jesus appears to rebuke him but, on a Gnostic reading, I think we must understand his words to mean: "I am not thy master because we are all of the same (divine) essence; you have learned your true nature from me and because of that you think of me as superior." Then Jesus takes him aside and speaks "secret words" which Thomas does not reveal. This is a favorite Gnostic device and we may suppose that many different versions of the three words existed. On the other hand Thomas does say that if he were to reveal one of the words the other disciples would stone him. This reminds us of John 8:58–59 and John 10:30–31 where, because Jesus says, respectively, "I am" and "I and the Father are one," the Jews take up stones to stone him. In both these Johannine passages Jesus is claiming identity with Yahweh. Something like this may well be implied here and if so it indicates the "mixed" background of this work.

The final question and answer are taken from the *Gospel of Thomas* and are a reminiscence of the synoptic sayings in which Jesus states that we shall know the tree from its fruit and both are either good or bad. The Jews are unable to perceive this because they have been deceived by the god of creation and it is for this reason that they cannot recognize Jesus either. This is at least a possible interpretation of this rather difficult logion.

The Action of Judas Iscariot

This excerpt is a hypothetical reconstruction based on existing information about a lost *Gospel of Judas*. Our information about this gospel and the Christian Gnostic sect to which it is attributed (the "Cainites") comes from Irenaeus (second century), Tertullian (early third century) and Epiphanius (fourth century). According to Irenaeus the Cainites maintained that a knowledge of the true God was the preserve of all those Old Testament figures who are presented, in the Bible, as being wicked (e.g., Cain, Esau, Korah, the Sodomites) and reprobate. Judas, "alone of all the apostles," knew that Jesus had been sent by the true God and that (Tertullian) "the powers of this world did not wish Christ to suffer that salvation might not be given to the human race." Therefore (Irenaeus again) he "accomplished the mystery of the betrayal, by which everything earthly and heavenly is dissolved, as they say." This excerpt has been put together with relevant texts from the canonical Gospels (John 11:48; Mark

14:1–2; 1 John 5:19; John 12:31–32; John 13:27), and the fragmentary information deriving from our ancient sources.

It is important to realize that although the Gnostics made abundant use of the Old Testament they regarded the God of Moses as an imposter, sometimes as a malevolent imposter and sometimes merely as an ignorant one. The simplest way of explaining this is by saying that they looked upon the material world as the source of man's suffering. Most (not all) men are born with a spark of the divine, but they are unaware of this. From eternity the true God has given birth to emanations, the most junior of which (usually characterized as *Sophia* a female principle), being so far removed from the Father, made the mistake of creating and was, as a consequence, embroiled herself in the world of matter. One of her creatures was the God of the Hebrews, Yahweh. Man can be "saved" only if he comes to realize that he is a fragment, as it were, of Sophia, and he can only know this if it is revealed to him by a heaven-sent messenger (such as Jesus).

The Last Supper

Except for the reference to Mary Magdalene's laughter this excerpt is once again taken from the *Acts of John*. The few lines about Mary come from the *Apostolic Church Order* and they are so strange, so much more suited to a Gnostic context, that I have included them here. In the source Martha explains that Mary was laughing (or smiling) because she remembered the words of Jesus: "What is weak will be saved by means of what is strong," but this makes no sense at all in a Last Supper setting and we can, I think, be reasonably sure that we have here a fragment from a Last Supper narrative in which Mary Magdalene played a significant role.

The reference to the "lawless Jews" who had their "Law" from the "lawless serpent" can be read as anti-

Jewish polemic, which to some extent it probably is (one thinks of the words of Jesus at John 8:44: "you are from your father the devil"), but for the Gnostic the primary attack is on the *origin* of Jewish religion: Yahweh, who gave the "Law," is the creator of this world. Both the act of creation and the giving of the Law are born of ignorance and contrary to the will of the true Father whom the god of the Jews does not know. The Jews are "lawless" in the same sense as the serpent (who is here identified with Yahweh) because the "Law," which the one gives and the others receive, is in reality no law at all.

The Choral dance has long been viewed as a curiosity. Jesus dancing in a circle with his disciples seems bizarre. However, it is quite likely that in some Jewish communities at least, dancing was part of the Passover ritual (cp. W. C. Van Unnik: "A Note on the Dance of Jesus in the 'Acts of John,'" *Vigiliae Christianae* 18, 1964, pp. 1–5), and in the view of a number of scholars the central element in the earliest Passover ritual was a limping dance (cp. T. H. Gaster: *Passover: Its History and Traditions* [New York, 1949], esp. pp. 23–25). We note that nothing is said here about the Passover meal, which is the focal point of the synoptic accounts. In the Fourth Gospel, however, the meal is only alluded to (John 13:2, 4, 18, 26, 30), and the interest of this evangelist is in the foot-washing ceremony and the long discourse of Jesus which begins at 13:31 and continues through chapter 17. The hymn which Jesus sings in these *Acts* (cp. Mark 14:26; Matt. 26:30) takes the place of the Johannine discourse. There appear to be a number of allusions to Johannine language in this hymn: Jesus would be "eaten" (cp. John 6:53), "heard" (cp. John 5:24–29), would "wash" (John 13:8), has "houses" and "places" (cp. John 14:2), is a "lamp" (cp. John 5:3; Apoc. 21:23), a "door" (John 10:9), a "way" (John 14:6), would "be united" and "unite" (John 17:29–21) and only here and in 1 John 1:5 is God called "Light" in whom is no darkness. There are, as well, some very specific Gnostic references: "The number Eight" and "the number Twelve" are to be understood as the emanations of the divine substance which play so large a role in Gnostic cosmologies. When Jesus says to the disciples, as he does here, that "thou couldest not at all have understood what thou sufferest if I had not been sent unto thee" he is speaking as the archetypal Gnostic redeemer come to teach men how to escape from suffering. Note, too, the statement: "What now I am seen to be, that I am not." This is capable of an "orthodox" interpretation.

I have added, at what seems a most appropriate place, the disciples' question about their own end. This is another saying from the *Gospel of Thomas*. Jesus, in very Johannine fashion, does not answer their question but alludes to the Gnostic preoccupation with the end— reconciliation in the *Pleroma*—being the beginning. In the synoptic Gospels also the disciples ask Jesus about the end of the world but his response, though almost as evasive, is nothing like this.

Crucifixion and Appearance to John

This excerpt follows immediately upon the choral dance section in the *Acts of John*. This author agrees with Mark 14:50 and Matt. 26:56 in stating that the disciples fled from Jesus. In the Fourth Gospel, however, the beloved disciple, John, follows Jesus to his crucifixion and alone of all stands by the cross to the end (John 19:26–27). In this passage John also flees but he has a privileged encounter with Jesus from which it emerges that the Lord only appeared to suffer and die on the cross. There is some similarity here with what Irenaeus tells us Basilides taught, namely that on the way to Golgotha Jesus switched places with Simon of Cyrene (cp. Mark 15:21–22) and stood and mocked the Jews while Simon hung on the cross, but here there is no hint that Jesus has effected a substitution, only the revelation that what he is he alone knows and what other men perceive (like the Jews below on Calvary) is illusory.

It is worth noting that in the Fourth Gospel the first appearance of Jesus is to Mary Magdalene whereas here it is to John; just the reverse of what we would expect in the light of earlier comments on the Gnostic esteem for Mary.

Ascension and Going Forth of the Apostles

This final episode which may be compared to Matt. 28:16–20 and Acts 1:6–11, comes from the fragmentary *Gospel of Mary* a Gnostic work discovered in the previous century and thought to date from the second century (*see* R. M. Grant: *Gnosticism* [New York, 1961], p. 63). Unfortunately we cannot make much of the secret teaching Mary imparts to the disciples because several leaves of the gospel are missing at just this point. It seems to have dealt, generally, with the plight of the soul, its struggles and its final ascent to glory. What is much more interesting to us is the re-action of the disciples who find this teaching unlike anything they remember hearing from Jesus. The demur is voiced by Peter and Andrew, the two senior apostles. Levi, interestingly, intervenes and restores harmony. This strongly suggests the kind of situation which characterized Christianity in the second century: the conflict between those who claimed to teach the authentic and "orthodox" faith and those (Gnostics) who claimed to teach the secret but equally authentic faith. Mary represents Gnosticism here; Andrew and Peter the more traditional Jewish Christianity. Levi perhaps represents the church of Syria (whence Matthew's Gospel, the letters of Ignatius, etc.) where, during the second century Gnosticism appears to have made significant inroads. In one way or other Bardesanes, the author of the *Odes of Solomon* and even Ignatius himself reflect Gnostic tendencies. Our little story may be a reminiscence of the Syrian church's attempt to mediate between the two parties.

Evangelist's Epilogue

This epilogue is taken from *The Gospel of Truth* and follows, by some thirty lines, the little gospel summary which we read in the section *The Beginning of the Public Ministry*; it is representative of the occasional outbursts of feeling which constitute the best literary portions of this gospel. In content these few lines remind us of Colossians 2:14: "having cancelled the bond which stood against us with its legal demands; this he set aside, nailing it to the cross." No doubt the author of *The Gospel of Truth* is thinking of that passage, but he sees the "testamentary disposition" which Jesus nails to the Cross as the affirmation of the Father's love for us, not as the Law because of which we have all become guilty. Unlike the author of the *Acts of John*, this author (Valentinus?) accepts the death of Jesus on the cross as a reality although he shows his Gnostic bent in his reference to the human nature of Jesus as "rags."